C000235275

The Lazy
Optimist

To Jules

Enjoy ☺

[signature]

The Lazy
Optimist

Waking up from mediocrity & turning dreams into reality

MARTIN GLADDISH

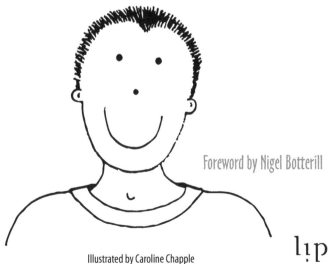

Foreword by Nigel Botterill

Illustrated by Caroline Chapple

lip

First published in 2013 by:

Live It Publishing
27 Old Gloucester Road
London, United Kingdom.
WC1N 3AX
www.liveitpublishing.com

Copyright © 2013 by Martin Gladdish

The moral right of Martin Gladdish to be identified as the author
of this work has been asserted by him in accordance with the
Copyright, Designs and Patents Act 1988.

All rights reserved.

Except as permitted under current legislation, no part of this
work may be photocopied, stored in a retrieval system,
published, performed in public, adapted, broadcast,
transmitted, recorded or reproduced in any form or by any
means, without the prior permission of the copyright owners.

All enquiries should be addressed to Live It Publishing.

ISBN 978-1-906954-72-7

To Emma: for putting up with my hopes
and dreams and also fulfilling them

Acknowledgements

Where do you start and how far back do you go in saying thanks? Well this book, as anyone that knows me well could tell you, has been a frustrated element of my life for longer than I will admit; and anyone who reads the book will understand why. But it was meeting Nigel Botterill (who has now become a great business mentor for me) that finally spurred me on to getting it done; so thank you Nigel. Big thanks also goes to Louise Heasman and Murielle Maupoint who said just the right things to give me the confidence I needed to finish what had previously been a series of false starts. Murielle, founder of Live It Publishing, then proceeded to orchestrate the creation of this fine collection of pages you hold in your hand. I would also like to thank Sarah and Tanju, my two school teacher friends, who kindly gave up their time to read though the manuscript for me and assure me that I wasn't going mad. Finally, I would like to thank my parents more than I can say for giving me such a safe and solid start in life and creating a dependable foundation which gave a desperate daydreamer a half decent chance of getting somewhere… oh, and for taking him on truly wonderful childhood holidays ;-)

"If someone is going down the wrong road, he doesn't need motivation to speed him up. What he needs is education to turn him around"

Jim Rohn

Foreword

When Martin Gladdish told me he was planning to write a book called "The Lazy Optimist" I took it with a pinch of salt. Nice title, I thought, I wonder if he'll ever get it finished.

Don't get me wrong, my doubts as to whether this book would ever be completed were much less to do with Martin and much more to do with the plethora of other people who have told me, in recent times, about their plans to write a book. The truth is, in most cases, it never happens. And, in the same way, those same people and millions more like them, go through life with wishes, dreams and ambitions that all sound great but somehow never materialise or come to fruition.

What Martin has done in this book, quite brilliantly at times, is explain why that it is.

He has cut through all the psychobabble and jargon and identified in his own inimitable style why most people are not living the life that they dreamed they would as a child and, more importantly, how to fix that.

I am not pretending, and Martin will be the first to insist, that simply reading this book will not change your life but it will provide you with a profound insight and some practical steps to do something about it, if you so wish.

If, like me, you collected football stickers in your youth then you simply have to read this book to understand how the gaps in your Panini album when you were only 11 years of age was in fact a metaphor for your whole life…

Martin, I salute you. You have grappled with one of the big issues of our time and you've come out on top. You've produced a book which, for me, ticks the three most important elements:-

- It's genuinely interesting…
- It's really useful…
- It can be read, in its entirety, in less than 90 minutes

Much respect.

Nigel Botterill
Multi-award winning UK entrepreneur
Sunday Times bestselling author
January 2013

Chapter 1

Charlie starts to dream…

Charlie believed that he was going to be successful. He believed that he was special and that 'one day' he would rise above the mass of mediocrity which surrounded him, dragged him down and slowly drained him of his ambition; and then he would make a name for himself. He had always believed that success was an inescapable part of his future because Charlie had seized hold of a dream; and in this bright and colourful vision of his own destiny he saw himself winning. It had always been part of his nature to see life this way. To look beyond his present circumstances and see that tomorrow everything would be better; much, much better. Charlie supposed that this was because he was one of those fortunate people in life who just happened to be a natural optimist.

Later in life Charlie would have a bookshelf full of books about the power of positive thinking and the importance of imagining yourself being successful. These books (some of which he had even read) would add fuel to his dream and keep its embers burning long after the hopes of an ordinary, pessimistic man would have dwindled into darkness. Occasionally, he would look back on his life of desire and, with his library of dreams as a backdrop, he would picture each and every hope he had ever had; sometimes bright, sometimes a shimmering mirage, but each one a declaration of his state of mind. He was an unmoveable, undeniable, unshakeable, totally unmistakeable optimist.

Charlie first identified his gift for seeing a brighter future one evening after school, shortly before his eleventh birthday. It started when his Mum brought home the latest football sticker album and two packets of stickers as a reward for having helped his Dad with the gardening the previous weekend. He was delighted to be a part of this new adventure which he had previously watched from a disinterested distance spread like a rumour around the playground. Soon he became hooked, as he slowly evolved into an avid collector and finally developed a single-minded determination, driven from the very centre of his heart, to complete the set by the end of the season. At first Charlie was simply excited at the idea of being part of the 'popular-kids' conversation at break-times; discussing his growing collection and comparing notes with his friends whilst remaining totally focussed on the prospect of reaching his own personal target. As time went on and the season progressed past the busy Christmas fixtures he became nothing short of obsessed and was completely absorbed in the chase. The competition to achieve was heightened and the relationship with some of his friends tightened, as he set his attention on reaching not only his own goal, but also fulfilling his newly awakened need to be seen as a winner amongst his peers. Every penny he could find; the change from his lunch money and every fee-earning chore he was offered, contributed to one more packet of sticky-back pictures of football players. At some point, a month or so before the close of that year's football season (Charlie hardly even noticed it happen), he started to envy some of the other boys in his class whose parents were more generous with their pocket money and who always seemed to have more 'swapsies' to trade with. He would watch them from his desk during lessons and wondered how it was that those same boys always seemed to find all the rarest stickers while he ended up feeling totally dejected with a bag full of 'doubles' and odd empty spaces on dog-eared pages.

Charlie sometimes wondered what happened to his collection of 'almost finished' football sticker albums…

Charlie's best friend at school had an older brother who played lead guitar in a local rock band, 'The Shock Grenades', and sometimes they would sneak into his room when he was out and pretend they were on 'Top of the Pops'. They would imagine setting the music world alight with their own unique sound, driving fancy sports cars, embarking on world tours and playing to sell-out crowds in Wembley Stadium. They would practice signing autographs on spare pages in last year's school books, bowing before the Queen on opening night at the Palladium and dreaming of all the things they would do with the huge sums of money they would inevitably be earning. Eventually Charlie asked his parents for a guitar of his own and spent the next two months composing a rhythmic melody of pleading, begging and offering to do extra chores around the house and in the garden. This continual beating of his wholehearted desire to invest in a dream seemed to fill the house with music; and as the tune became more familiar and showed no signs of retreating down the charts he slowly wore down their resistance to its sound. No one could ever question Charlie's unwavering determination to start a project and when he came home one day with a form applying to join the after-school music club they finally relented and he got his first guitar – an unbranded (but well researched, reasonably good quality) nylon-stringed acoustic in a thin canvas case.

You could not have imagined a happier boy. He was playing basic songs in no time, showing an interest in his Dad's old record collection and practicing almost every night. To say that he had natural talent and a real ear for music would have been an understatement. Charlie truly shone and his music reports reflected the glow. His friend soon went off the idea, probably because his big brother had now moved out of home and stopped paying him any attention, but for Charlie it was different. He had discovered a talent which he knew with every fibre of his being was going to play a large part in his future. He had made contact with an inner passion for music which few others knew, or could ever hope to understand. This revelation lit the touch paper to a furnace deep within his heart which would one day burn bright enough for the whole world to see. He was going to achieve fame and fortune and fulfil an array of dreams, ambitions and goals which he could only even start to imagine. Needless to say Charlie never had any doubt that his talent would lead him into the lap of success which occupied his music filled imaginings each night. At school concerts he would scan the crowd looking for unfamiliar faces in flat caps, scouting out the next big thing; and he often listened to the radio with great anticipation, expecting to hear his name celebrated across the airwaves 'Charlie – new in at number four'. Once he even penned a letter to a record company, together with a demo tape recorded in secret in his bedroom; a creative cover of an old Beatles classic.

Charlie forgot how many times he had dropped that recording into his school bag with every intention of letting it fall into the red letterbox which he passed each day as he cycled to school. In the end he persuaded himself that the chance of his precious, priceless dream getting stuck in the corner of that big red bottomless box or falling into the hands of an evil producer who would pass it off as his own was far too big a risk to take. The letter along with the tape ended up at the bottom of a tatty old green shoebox containing other treasures, hopes and dreams from the early life of this born optimist.

Charlie went on to become one of the best guitar players in the school, performing in many recitals, concerts and plays. In his final year he was selected to represent his entire school in a regional talent show where he won third prize in his age category and in all truth could quite easily have taken the top prize. He was invited back the following year to compete in the under eighteens group but he issued his response in defiant absence; by not even turning up to the heats. But Charlie's Mum was so proud when one of his very own compositions was used at the school's 'twenty fifth anniversary' celebration. And the commemorative certificate that they gave him sat on her mantelpiece for years afterwards and may even still be there to this day, slightly faded but still a shade or two brighter than Charlie's promising music career.

Johnny Dawson, one of the boys in Charlie's class, went to Florida the following summer holiday. He brought back some American chocolate which he shared with the whole class, two packs of glossy photographs and some exciting stories full of fun-filled fantasy and roller-coaster rides. Apparently the sun shines all day in Florida and the ice creams are about three times the size of the ones that you get at your average English seaside resort. In that land of extravagance and opportunity they eat pancakes for breakfast, steak and chips for lunch and most of the cars are bigger than a Rolls Royce. Charlie and his family had been to Swanage again that year and stayed in a tent on a campsite, next to a dairy farm with its own little shop supplying the daily needs of the campers and a few plastic toys for the beach. The site was about a mile from the seaside and a good fifty yards from the cold, wet, spider-web filled toilet block. It was fairly sunny most of that week, apart from the night when the tent leaked, and the wasp problem wasn't nearly as bad as it had been the previous year. He had enjoyed making friends with the other kids staying on the campsite, going down to the beach, swimming and playing swing-tennis and football. He spent most of his mornings delightfully engrossed amongst the rock-pools looking for crabs, gobies and blennies, where he decided that being a marine biologist might be a great career for a talented and knowledgeable enthusiast such as himself. Somewhere in his mind he held on to the exciting hope that he might just discover a new species that morning and hit the headlines as a famous explorer, complete with the accompanying fame and fortune. But he never did.

The whole family would sit down together in the evenings, talking, laughing and enjoying their fish and chips. Those were immensely contented times which made Charlie realise what a wonderful life he had. One night he made a wish that such days of happy togetherness would last forever, when he and his Dad saw a shooting star whizz silently across the blanket of dreams which hung overhead.

Each night of that holiday, in a simple campsite in Swanage, Charlie drifted into blissful sleep wrapped up in the warmest of thoughts. He was surrounded by and absolutely secure in the knowledge that those who loved him most were only a canvas wall away and he was certain that he was the luckiest kid in the world having the best holiday ever.

Charlie never talked about his holidays that year when he got back to school. It seemed that his memories were never quite as bright as the other kid's, and whilst he still loved his family, and he knew that they loved him, he felt he would always need a little bit more. In Charlie's mind, although he never told anyone, he began to believe that he had been to Florida, and that he had been given his own ice cream shop where people would be queuing along the beach, just to sample the fabulous flavours he had invented. On one occasion whilst he was walking through Disneyland he had been given a ticket which entitled him to priority entry onto all of the rides ahead of everyone else and let him buy anything he liked from the gift shops. Charlie began looking forward to next summer when, perhaps, the whole family would be able to go to Florida with him again… because Charlie was determined that his life would be a success; and why shouldn't it be? After all he was a natural optimist and he knew with all the certainty of a 'wish upon a star' that he was special.

Destiny was on his side. It was his most loyal ally and one day, somewhere, somehow he would find his place very close to the top of the world. There was no way that Charlie would be, or even possibly could be, anything other than a complete success; his dream would never ever die.

One day, not too long after he had celebrated his fourteenth birthday with a shiny new bike, Charlie overheard two boys discussing the things they were planning to buy with all the money they made from various paper rounds at the local newsagents. One of them claimed to have made six pounds for delivering papers for just two evenings each week. This news was like someone banging furiously on the front door of Charlie's life; barging in without even waiting for him to answer. Then switching all the lights on at once, shouting 'surprise' in a very loud voice and setting off a load of turbo-charged, brightly coloured party-poppers. It was a complete and total revelation! Maybe he could earn his own money too! Why had no one told him about this before? This could be his ticket out of the 'ordinary boys' league and into the popular classes. Was it possible that this was actually it; the thing which could launch his life of achievement and endless golden opportunities? He could mix with those boys that bought sweets everyday and shared them without a care. He would have the best football boots, trendy clothes and the very latest, super-alloy BMX; he would be rich.

Driven by a desire to get closer to success Charlie worked incredibly hard in his new found employment. He had taken the shop manager by complete surprise at the enthusiasm he demonstrated in taking on his early morning round; getting up with the birds, cycling to the shop and delivering every paper without a single error; he did just great. With an incredible sense of fulfilment, a full fifteen pounds a week was his reward, plus three more for each of the extra rounds he covered, from time to time. Charlie was in his element and the more he engaged with the world of work the more his mind began to get carried away with the opportunities to advance. He would become a big business man, build a busy factory where he would sit in his extravagant office behind a huge oak desk on a big leather chair; and create an international corporate empire to dominate its marketplace.

Nothing could stop his passion-fuelled ambition. He was soon promoted to be the boy that organised the other rounds, an amazing twenty five pounds a week;

and a few years later he also stood behind the cashier's till in the evenings after college. As his studies continued, so did his hard-working, cash generating ventures; spending, saving striving and dreaming whilst enjoying the freedom and perks of his newly discovered, but well-earned wealth. He would confidently, without a single hint of arrogance, tell his parents and all of their friends that he would drive a Ferrari by the age of twenty-one and he genuinely believed these words to be true. You see Charlie was a natural optimist.

Charlie had always believed that he was going to be successful and towards the end of his childhood, at that time when the dreams of most people tend to fade silently from view or are snatched away by the harshness of life, Charlie's hope still burned brightly. Despite his disappointments and failures, most of which he had banished to a corner of his mind that he refused to visit, he knew that his dreams really would come true. Subconsciously he still understood that he was special and that one day he would make contact with the destiny which beckoned him. And as he left behind his meagre education and moved into young adulthood he had discovered that working hard brought its own reward and this drove him on to be a diligent (but sometimes distant) employee for many years to come.

This revelation had ignited his youthful, fanciful, hope-filled dreams and fired up his ambition.

And so the cruel, cancerous and cleverly disguised illusion of success began to grow and flourish in the innocent mind of a natural-born, enthusiastic and hardworking optimist… but one who was certainly not alone in suffering from this condition.

"Dreams, discoveries and the desire to reach them will fuel your ambitions"

Chapter 2

Charlie has a lie-in…

By the time Charlie left school he was firmly established as one of the higher salary earners amongst his peers and was immensely proud of his place in the world. He still dreamed of his Ferrari and had added: running his own successful business empire, marrying a beautiful wife, buying a holiday home in the sun and being a multi-millionaire to the colourful, crisp image that held centre stage in his mind… All by the time he was twenty-one.

Charlie continued to work hard as he made his way into his post 'football stickers and paper rounds' life; rising early, working late and playing hard. Even when he wrote off his bike one morning, breaking several bones, he simply took on more hours in the store behind the till and the cash continued to flow; nothing would curb his hunger to work. He left college midway through his first term; bored by the slow monotony of the classroom and eager to get into the workforce and make his fortune as soon as possible. He got a job as a printing apprentice. The phrase "the world will always need printers" indelibly published upon his mind for many years to come. The thrill of learning a genuine skill, an honourable trade which was more akin to an art form, and one which only those with an eye for precision and colour could master. Like an alchemist creating gold from base metal, Charlie would get lost in the delight of printing a menagerie of information in glorious four-colour finishes onto various substrates; from heavy bond and quality boards to glossy, matt and silk papers, all stacked neatly at the end of his Heidelberg GTO. He was quickly becoming a master in his craft, creating beautiful work and generating income; all in the name of optimism and the journey towards a dream which lingered somewhere in the dimly lit space between his heart and his mind. Such was his drive and passion for success and to earn the mountains of money that would give life to his goals that he still worked three evenings a week behind the counter in the paper shop (which had since evolved into a convenience store).

No one could ever say that Charlie didn't work hard, that he didn't deserve a break and that he wouldn't go far; and no one could ever doubt the conviction behind his ambition.

Relishing the empowering feeling that he was doing something right (he had to be, because he was always busy) Charlie pushed himself further, dug himself deeper; huffed and puffed and smiled and sighed… Nothing could diminish his fervour for working hard.

Nothing could take away his addiction to 'putting in the hours' or remove his head from the sandpit of busyness in which it was buried and which had begun to dominate every moment of his life.

Twenty-one came and went and although the dream was still there (floating, less bright but still alive, somewhere behind a stack of stress and hidden amidst a sea of overtime hours in a distant corner of his mind) Charlie barely noticed that his dreamline-deadline had ticked its final tock.

In the years that followed Charlie became a serial job-hopper, addicted to betterment, working hard, slogging along and occasionally enjoying the fruit of his labour as he settled into his ordinary life. Each new appointment brought hope; an ocean of promise, the chance to impress, the chase for promotion and the opportunity to place his feet firmly upon the next rung of the ladder and don the mantle of success. Wherever Charlie went he did OK, he sparkled but never quiet shone, he got noticed but just didn't seem to ever make his mark. He became a so-so achiever; not rich, not poor, dreaming from time to time and denying the passive passing of his years.

If you had met Charlie in those days and asked him how things were going he would have convinced you that everything was fantastic. He would have told you that life was great; he would have shared his plans for an exciting cruise or tour of distant lands. He would have described the new car that would soon be on order and how it was almost certain that he would be offered a new role in a more senior position at work during the next quarter. What's more, you would have almost certainly believed him. That's because Charlie believed everything he said and thought; not just on the surface but driven from the deepest part of his heart he knew that he was destined for greatness and, as a natural optimist, it was this conviction that he vibrantly displayed to the world. This mirage, created by Charlie's vivid and brilliant imagination, was also what he saw when he looked in the mirror each day and was an outward manifestation of the inward affliction which had taken root in his heart and which was wilfully manipulating the very rhythm of his life.

You see Charlie, like so many other ordinary people, suffered from a very common, yet little known and rarely diagnosed condition called 'lazy optimism'. This highly deceptive and mischievous affliction attaches itself to an imagination (often from a young age) and stirs up achievable allusions of grandeur and success. It then enters a stage of sitting quietly dormant, sometimes for years, before proceeding to slowly and subtly move those dreams just in sight, but painfully beyond reach. It does this by misdirection and sleight of mind in the same way that a magician will convince you that the card you picked was the one you merely thought of; and the rope you just cut is the same one he still holds in his dexterous and tricky hands. This belief is then further enforced by the kindly meant, but equally erroneous, encouragement of others to keep slogging away until Lady Luck smiles upon the sufferer's endeavour. In all but the most serious of cases of 'lazy optimism' the main cause is that its victim once came into direct contact with the misguided, but seemingly logical, idea that being enthusiastically busy is the way to achieve the dreams and desires of a lifetime.

Like any astounding and attractive magic trick (or dare I say lie) the power of its wonder is increased by its subtly accurate representation of the truth; and its fire is fuelled all the more by the willingness of its audience to believe. At this point in Charlie's life he didn't realise that this was why he was always chasing; but it is good for you to know some of the symptoms of this cruel affliction at this point in his story.

Despite the frantic lifestyle he had created for himself, there were still times when Charlie would stop and ponder his life and wonder when he would get a glimpse of his rightful destination. This was because he still believed that one day he was going to be successful; he believed that he was special and that he would make it in the end. The dream lived on; a bit blurred at its edges, fuzzy in the middle and distinctly void of the colour which had once illuminated its substance; but he would get there, he would revive, survive and thrive. Charlie was still absolutely convinced that he was one of life's natural optimists and that meant he would always be able to rise above the disappointments and dead ends which had so often tarnished his way. For this fact he supposed he would always be grateful; but it was behind this desperately delusional belief that he chose to hide for many more years to come.

There is not too much more to say about the chapter in Charlie's life where he became numb to his dreams and chose instead the distractions and allures of security, stability, practicality and hopeful longevity. In short he became just like everyone else; optimists, pessimists, dreamers and realists alike; fighting in the rat race, keeping up with the Joneses and pounding out an ever deeper rut to march along each day. He joined the mass of individuals that populate the civilized world, labouring through, following the crowd and unwittingly paying for the privilege at the bitter cost of their dreams. In summary, Charlie's daily chasing of his tail was accompanied by the same highlights and lowlights that flavour the lives of other ordinary people. He became a husband and then a dad; he lost loved ones and made friends; he bought a mortgage, a house and a car; he laughed and he cried; he became just another man in the street. In fact, if the truth be told (when measured against the average man of his peers) Charlie had a good life where the sunshine shone more often than the rainfall fell. And compared to the sufferings and poverty of those whose situations people like Charlie justified with a phone call on the odd Friday night in front of a celebrity filled TV screen, he had a great life; a veritable lap of luxury… But it was still an out and out denial of the dream which was suffocating behind his inability to see beyond an illusion.

You see, Charlie had in fact made a decision about his life. It was an unconscious one, made in total innocence, but it was his decision all the same. The reality was that he had no one else to blame. Charlie had chosen to defer his life to its default setting of 'ordinary man' simply by not having the courage to move the dial round a few notches to 'dream achiever'. He didn't have to do this; he'd been glimpsing the dream out of the corner of his eye most of his life, and it had danced through his mind almost every night as he slept in comfortable, lazy, escapism. But it was still categorically his decision.

He occasionally crossed the paths of those that represented his dream and whilst he was always polite and afforded them a genuine air of respect, deep inside him a fiery jealously raged. Why had they been lucky enough to take hold of his dreams? What gave them the right?

Not all of these people were fabulously rich, super-cool and famous or even individuals that had made a difference (although some of them were) but they all had 'something'. They confidently walked through each day with their heads well clear of the parapet that your average person chose to live behind. They didn't fear being shot at for their boldness or being told to get down. They weren't necessarily arrogant or proud (although some of them were) but they all had 'something'. Many of these people were really successful in businesses; some were authors or spent half their time abroad; others had found genuine peace through faith in God or somehow worked for the joy of it and not the 'want'. In Charlie's eyes they seemed to have stopped trying and started achieving; like a kind of 'optimism in action'. But it appeared to Charlie that whatever he tried never quite seemed to satisfy the yearning in his heart that those 'lucky' people had stumbled across. This was, of course, a total misdiagnoses of the situation on Charlie's part because there was something very different between these people and him. They knew the secret ingredient that turned optimism from a curse into a blessing; they knew that simply wanting something would never be enough. Optimism is the easy bit; anybody can want success; but it takes genuine courage and the right sort of effort to really make things happen.

Sitting on the train to work Charlie would watch those around him, trying to identify the frauds and the fakers and deflect the attention from the apathy he'd started using to keep him warm at the start of each day. It would usually be crowded when he boarded the train, but on this particular morning he spotted a space and went to sit down next to a tired looking gentleman whose general shape had either been forgotten or ignored by the people who make train seats. Charlie angled his legs back towards the aisle, brushing past the knees of the sleeping lady opposite, who opened one eye for a moment before returning to her semiconscious doze. The man next to her gazed pensively into the space above Charlie's left shoulder as if he was expecting to find something, perhaps a loved one or the answer to a matter of impending doom. Charlie found himself counting to see how long it would be until the man blinked before his attention was briefly drawn back to the sleeping lady. People shouldn't yawn on trains or do any other facial exercises. It's not very attractive.

The big guy next door shifted his considerable frame slightly, causing Charlie to readjust his position further into the aisle. Feeling vaguely comfortable again he looked back at the staring man who obviously hadn't found anything yet because he was still looking. About mid to late 40's with a less than generous crop of loose grey hair and it appeared that his forehead had gained an extra wrinkle since the last time he looked. His suit and overcoat said he was a confident achiever, a man of means and not afraid to use them. But his eyes betrayed him, revealing an insight into a different soul, and the way his lightly clasped hands fidgeted with the handle of the slim-line briefcase on his lap exposed him as merely mortal and troubled by the thought. The train stopped and simultaneously a look of sheer determined confidence swept across his face as he stood and left behind a part of him which perhaps existed only on the train. Meanwhile Charlie's neighbour slept on, disturbed only momentarily by another traveller adding her personality to his day and filling the now vacant seat before him. He'd seen her before (you remember people like that) big red-rimmed glasses and a nose not so much buried as glued to her book. She was fairly small and had an almost awed look on her face, mostly due, to her living every spare moment of her day in a world of total make-believe. Awe turned to a gentle smile as she appeared to be touched by some comment in the book and she eagerly reached for the next page, hardly even noticing the volcano blowing his nose next to Charlie. Etiquette would suggest that a simple wipe would suffice, but perhaps he was being picky.

His attention was then drawn to another familiar face, middle-aged and dressed in grey she settled across the train; her face betraying deep sorrow as though in the midst of a great trial. Vaguely aware of others around her she stared out of the window, a hint of dampness resting at the tender edge of her eyes. These were eyes like deep pools of regret that told a story so sad they seemed to suck you in to their despair. As her head drifted slowly to one side, her hand moved in sync to support it and there she remained, looking at a world void of hope through a dirty old window, decorated by a worn out no smoking sign. At the next stop the 'more than regular' gentleman beside Charlie hoisted himself up and left, making way for the ultimate city stereotype; his pinstripes declaring loud and clear that he would normally take a taxi but as a one-off he decided to mix with the lower classes. This lie, however, was also equally lost within the plethora of deceptions and performances that are on display in the lives of the millions of ordinary people that suffer with lazy optimism. But this guy was a real pro as he drew the Financial Times from his brown leather briefcase then skilfully folded it into quarters before reading it through the bottom of his designer specs. As the train entered the tunnel which took them to its final stop Charlie's attention was drawn to another man trying to escape some deep rooted challenge which had obviously plagued him for years. He continued to stare at this mirage trying to work him out before noticing what appeared to be a tear beginning to build in the corner of his eye. This face faded behind a dirty window, Charlie wiped his cheek and made his way to work.

It was during this long period of slumber in his life that Charlie became familiar with the uncomfortable thought that perhaps he was just like everyone else after all. Deep down he knew that he was an optimist and that one day he was going to be successful. But over the years (which had somehow become decades) he increasingly questioned why it simply hadn't happened yet.

"A dream will only ever be a dream until you get it out of your head"

Chapter 3

Charlie wakes up…

One cold damp morning in October, around about a week before Charlie's fortieth birthday he awoke with a start… only to realise that he had completely stopped. His eyes were damp, the area behind his eyes throbbed and the luminous green numbers in front of him slowly came into focus and sluggishly transmitted the message through to his mind that it was mid-morning. He lay there another ten minutes trying to work out if it was Saturday or if he had booked a day out of the office, before coming to the conclusion that for the first time in his life he had overslept. Later his wife explained that he had mumbled something about feeling heavy and flat when she turned his alarm clock off three hours earlier; and so she had called work and made his excuses. That day Charlie began to think in a way in which he had never thought before. And by the end of that day he had added something to his thoughts that he had never really been brave enough to do before. He had started thinking with honesty.

He thought about his dream; he thought about his work; he thought about the people, just like him, that he saw on the train each morning. He thought about his future, his past, where he was now and just how much longer he might need to wait before he arrived where he wanted to be. He thought about his abilities, his strengths, his optimism, the effort that he applied to everything he had ever done and all the enthusiasm that he still believed he had to give. Charlie still desperately clung on to the belief that somewhere, just around the corner, an opportunity would present itself to him that would finally change his fortunes, put him on the map and make him into the success which he longed to become.

Whilst these thoughts whirled round his head that day he barely noticed anything else going on at all. The post remained unopened, as did the papers and he didn't even turn on the news. He barely ate because he was busy feeding on reminiscence and regret; but he did go into the loft to find his old guitar and, without hesitation, he began to strum. He was surprised at how easily his fingers found their way back to the strings and how readily chords, tunes and tempos returned. From 'blowing in the wind' and 'money for nothing' to the songs he played at school and those he composed in his own mind; he rediscovered some of his soul's rhythm that day. And as music has a propensity to influence a troubled mind he soon found himself drawn into pondering the lessons of yesteryear and wandering along memory muse.

Drifting in thought, lost in the moment and drawn deep into his mind's eye he gave in to his imagination. There he saw his old desk, worn down in the corners and scratched by years of playtimes and daydreams; and upon it a book of football stickers stretched open in front to him. He started to list the empty spaces as he turned each page; amazed at the pain such a worthless, tatty old book could still bring to his heart. He tried for a while to recall the name of the Dutch master, a real wizard with the ball at his feet, whose absence had been the final nail in that particular year's efforts. The smiles and hairstyles of his old friends' faces came into view and the warmth of school days and happy days combined into one as fond thoughts came rushing back. He began to think that life had been easy back then; everyone was equal and nothing really mattered all that much. Everyone he knew seemed to think this too; he had often teased his own nieces and nephews with patronising comments like 'you don't know how good you've got it' or 'wait until you enter the real world'. But the more his thoughts meandered the streets of his childhood and tip-toed through the corridors and classrooms of his old school the more he realised that back then things had really mattered; they had meant something.

When Charlie was younger he had believed in things, wanted things, strived for goals, stoked up the passion within himself that he could do anything he set his mind to. He had been an unshakeable, undeniable optimist. He began to see that the things which had always come easy to him; friendship, fun and day-dreaming were conjuring up happy thoughts. But the things which he never quite achieved, the beliefs beyond his reach had deposited pain in a bank of bitterness that had been gathering interest ever since. Whenever things didn't go quite his way, the way of someone who expected great things, he let disappointment lay down more roots. Charlie saw a happy childhood, in many ways a successful childhood; one where he worked hard, had lots of fun, and got off to a reasonably good start in life. But he also realised that he had blamed others every time something hadn't worked; that he would only sing when he was winning and always gave up when he wasn't.

He began to strum the melancholy opening bars of Pink Floyd's 'Wish You Were Here' and was once again sent spinning back into questioning life's indiscriminate inclination to deal an uneven hand. Why had he found it so difficult to enjoy his own achievements and appreciate the warmth and love of his family just because others seemed to have it better? How could it be that the best times of his childhood (days which inspired him, filled him with joy and gave him the confidence to believe in a dream) could be made to look so ordinary just because Johnny Dawson had been to Florida? And who could possibly deny that he deserved to get some luck soon; after all, hadn't he always been a hardworking optimist?

As his visions of childhood faded, along with the smells, sounds and sentimental stirrings of schooldays and holidays he began to think on his career and wondered why he had never quite seemed to get that lucky break. From cheerless early mornings on paper rounds battling the cold, the kerb and the heavy weight of daily news; through to late evenings behind a till being sneered at by his party bound friends. He'd spent a lifetime grafting; churning out work from his printing press through to scaling the corporate ladder in various city jobs just to find that circumstance had rung the changes against him once again. All his effort, the busy days, the overtime, the striving to achieve had never delivered on their promise and hard work had only ever let him down.

It was at this point that the idea arrived in front of Charlie's eyes, perhaps for the first time in his life, that he didn't even know what success looked like. He was sure that he did have a dream; and he knew that over the years he had imagined a whole bookshelf of very specific dreams, but he wasn't quite sure exactly what he would consider 'being successful' actually meant. He started to realise that his had been a life of genuine hope, held back by an invisible fear which was cunningly disguised as bad luck and resulting in a kind of directionless, busy-laziness. 'Busy' because Charlie had always worked hard, in most cases much, much harder than those around him; but 'lazy' because he had never really applied anything more than a half-hearted stab to pursuing the extraordinary. He was just like all of those people that he shared a journey with each morning on the train; those ordinary people with their ordinary lives and their fears, their features, their phobias and their flint-faced determination to simply carry on. He admired the guts and the resolve of the ordinary man and he wondered at his incredible ability to daily sit in a carriage with other individuals, just like him, pretending to be different but actually adding to the blend of the average person. It wasn't that Charlie had anything against the ordinary man, or that there was any shame in being average; in fact he recognised that that's what most people are. He just didn't want to be one of them anymore. He had never actually 'wanted' to be one of them in the first place; he had just unwittingly chosen that path by being too lazy to take the one sign-posted 'dreams'.

Charlie woke up to reality that day, the day on which he had overslept, and for the very first time in his life he began to see that simply believing in a dream would never ever be enough to actually start to build that dream in the real world. The reminiscing and the soul-searching had opened his eyes to the fact that he had been suffering from something more than just bad luck most of his life. But the diagnosis was not quite complete... that part was just about to happen.

After his day of reckoning which had started in despair and travelled across four decades to see a new understanding of his situation begin to emerge, he was actually feeling quite at ease with himself. So that afternoon, when his eleven year old son came in from school delighted to see that his dad was already at home, Charlie was in the perfect frame of mind to pay him more attention than usual as he cheerfully relayed the events of the day. He started with the journey to school and how much they had laughed when Elliott (his best friend) had almost fallen off his bike. The stories went into assembly and then the entertaining tale that Miss Rawlings had taught during their History lesson about two brothers who had wanted to learn how to fly. He enthusiastically re-enacted the stunning volley which he had scored at lunchtime to seal victory for his team over David Greene's and how some of the other boys had said it was one of the best goals they had ever seen. The highlight of his son's day, however, had been a lesson in the afternoon where they discussed their heroes and then went on to talk about the sort of jobs that they would like to do when they grew up. He mentioned seven or eight of his friends by name and their responses to this question, which included being a footballer, a doctor, a pop star, the Prime Minister and in the case of Elliott, the richest man in the world. Listening, but still half attached to his search for the absent dream that had held on to most of his mind all day Charlie was violently startled back to reality when his son asked him, "when did you know that you wanted to be a dispatch manager for a parcel company?"

Suddenly he could see it all; he had no control over who he had become.

All his life Charlie had believed that he was going to be successful; he believed that he was special and that one day he would make it. He had always believed this; he supposed that it was just part of his nature and that he was a natural optimist. But now he could see that he was actually afraid. He was afraid to become the dream, to touch the spark in his heart to its edges and see if it would flare into something beautiful or just flutter into the wind as ashes. He could see that he had made himself busy doing lots of things but this had simply been a distraction to stop him ever having to look his dreams in the face and make them happen. He had drifted throughout his entire life, paddling hard in the direction that he happened to be facing and ignoring the fact that he had access to the rudder. It wasn't that he couldn't be bothered but rather that he just wasn't bothered enough that he couldn't. He finally realised that he was an optimist: A lazy optimist. In fact he was just an ordinary man; simply a desperate dreamer swimming in a crowded world that was full of lazy optimists, just like him!

*"Don't just dream there…
do something"*

Chapter 4

Charlie looks in the mirror…

The following morning (this actually was a Saturday) Charlie looked in the mirror. And I don't mean just looked; he stared deeply, almost angrily at the man reflected back at him. He was still searching for something very specific but he didn't quite know what. At first he just saw skin, wrapped around the same structure that had housed his life for the past forty years. A very slightly receding hairline; refusing to completely give up the fight but struggling to provide any new material with which to present a case for staying. The unremarkable forehead, decorated by a single line, and behind which the weight of his world seemed to hang in the balance, churning in anticipation of a breakthrough but still prepared to go back into overdrive if that was the call. Below this his little upturned nose, broken (but barely noticeably) during a football match in his twenties; and either side of that cheeks that used to puff-up at the top when he smiled, but which now seemed held down with the heaviness of time. He considered the other features of his face for a while; familiar but older, worn and wearier, wiser perhaps, but certainly no better off for the influence. He continued to scan this portal into his soul for several minutes more; visiting scars, wrinkles and an unshaved chin; determined not to meet his own gaze.

Finally he arrived at his eyes, having avoided them for far longer than just this painful encounter, frightened of the tears that might be hiding behind their edges or the pain they might throw back at him. He explored those eyes looking for the thing that he had lost; the idea that had fuelled his childhood and catapulted him as a firework into life. The deeper he swam in this swirl of optical fluids before him, expecting to find something, the more he came to realise that hopes and dreams might just have a use by date; that they wouldn't wait around forever and that they probably had better things to do and more deserving people to present with their possibilities. In those eyes, however, Charlie still saw a glimmer of hope. He had seen it the day before too, but it wasn't until that moment that he realised how he may have been frightened all his life but that didn't mean he had to be frightened right now. He saw that the thing dreamers fear the most is that their dreams might let them down or, worse still, that they might not have it in them to meet their dreams' expectation. But what he also understood that day, as he allowed himself to confront his own heart with unguarded honesty, was that unless he was prepared to go for it, the dream would die anyway; so there genuinely was nothing to lose. He simply couldn't fail by trying; but he was absolutely certain to lose out if he didn't try at all.

Charlie looked in the mirror, hope looked back at him and hope said *"it is not too late to give life to your dreams; you just need to get them out of your head and into action"*.

Over that weekend Charlie switched off the whirling, whispering maelstrom of thoughts and experiences which had got him to this place; at the start of clarity with his good foot forward and on the road to giving life to his dreams. They had done their job; now it was down to him. He took a notebook and a pen; he went to his room, closed the door and he wrote down every hope that he had ever wished for or challenge that he'd wanted to pursue. The dull ones, the exciting ones, the sensible ones and the outrageously impossible ones; he listed them all. There were things he had already achieved and there were things he had forgotten he ever held dear; there were places he'd always wanted to go, songs he'd wanted to write and goals that had never made it past first base. He wrote down all his childhood unrealities, some whimsical possibilities, random thoughts and even some downright impossibilities; and then he went through them one by one and measured them against his heart. That day became the day that Charlie worked out the difference between simply wanting to achieve his dreams and actually pursuing them. Forty long hard years into his life, he finally understood that everyone 'wanted' to be successful and to fulfil their hearts desires; of course they did, that was normal. The hopes and dreams of the average person were only called hopes and dreams because they 'wanted' to achieve them. But to be different, to break the mould of normal, to be more than just a static optimist took something so much greater than simply wanting to do something. It meant grabbing hold of the things that you want with both hands, adding a little part of your heart, and taking those passions on a journey beyond simple desire and into places of action. He also learnt that whatever the desire might be it was the same obstacle which always stood in the way. And it wasn't circumstance, good luck or bad fortune as he had managed to convince himself all of his life. Sure they could have an effect on the individual and perhaps meant that everybody started out from a different place; but ultimately the barrier was in his own mind. It was him and his fear of not being able to achieve the things which he longed for; it was the laziness which had attached itself to his optimism. And it was only by finally being honest with himself that Charlie had realised that this was the thing which had become a blockade to his ambition. It was fear. And whilst fear is actually only a figment of an imagination, an impulsive but self-imposed reaction to a situation; in the real world it presents itself as lazy because it results in the death of positive action.

After Charlie had made his list he began to cross off anything written there which had stopped moving his heart; the ones which no longer stirred up the pain of regret and lost opportunity and those which perhaps provoked a memory and a smile, but nothing resembling heart's desire. This seemed the obvious thing to do simply because he was now looking from a different angle. A place where his optimism was only answerable to the desires of his heart today; and he surprised himself at just how easy this was to do and just how rewarding. This new man, the stronger, fresher faced man he saw the next time he looked in the mirror was certainly not the same one he had shared countless train journeys in ordinariness with in the past. As he drew a line through each of the things he had been afraid to do throughout his life he saw clarity swoop down and gently nestle alongside the treasures that remained. Then with strong claws and upon powerful wings those goals, those precious ideas, the pieces of his heart which still mattered to him today, were lifted off of the page and placed back in the spaces from where they had been taken; with new purpose and without fear.

He was finally ready to take action; and this is what he had learned along the way:

LESSON 1:
"Dreams, discoveries and the desire to reach them will fuel your ambitions"

Most children are free to dream and to imagine great things. It comes naturally to them and those who bring them up and influence their early years never tell them that they can't do the things that they desire or become the people that they want to be. This is because, whilst adults all too often forget how to dream themselves, some part of them still knows the power of an imagination and the value of vision. Indeed, the fantasies of youth are positively encouraged throughout our childhoods; fuelled by storybooks, fairy tales, cartoon characters and things to colour-in. But as we grow older, as we move beyond easy reach of a belief that we really could take hold of our ambitions; hope and optimism is infected by the seemingly rational ideas of averageness. Education, get a job, work hard, get married, buy a house, two-point-five children… join the system. Not that there is anything wrong with any of these things and Charlie certainly had no regrets about the loving family that he had been born into and had subsequently seen growing up around him. But he could now see that somewhere along the journey he had stopped believing in his dreams; and whilst the world around him, the ordinariness that seemed to permeate from almost everyone he had ever met, had been an influence; it was entirely his fault that he had let this happen. He had allowed the dream to grow and indulged himself in it as any child might; but as time moved on he became afraid and hid that dream behind the fraudulent excuse of simply being busy. He had slipped into the rut of ordinary and whilst his passion had still manifest itself in being a hard worker and striving to get 'somewhere' this route simply didn't have enough filling stations to fuel his aspirations, and get him to where he wanted to be.

The summary of Charlie's reflections as he looked back into his early years was that optimism itself was only enough to start the journey towards achievement and success (whatever that might mean to each individual heart). Fuelling this ambition was only as good as the direction in which the person had set their sights and the bravery and single-mindedness of their determination to stay on that track; regardless of distractions, failures and disappointments.

Most optimists are great starters, people with vision; but being an optimist is only half of the story. Plain old optimists are commonplace, average, ordinary people who are easily thrown off the track only to recover sometime later, place their hope on another vacant dream, and start again. Admirable qualities indeed and it is a marvel that there are so many optimists in the world that have the fortitude and will power to keep moving from one thing to another; seemingly resigned to the reality of never seeing a dream through to its end. But it's the finishers who win; the ones who are able to optimise their optimism, add belief and turn it into action. Successful optimists are those who are not content to let dreams slowly flicker into dullness, leaving them to linger painfully and pointlessly in dimly lit corners of their mind.

LESSON 2:
"A dream will only ever be a dream
until you get it out of your head"

Charlie was not a psychologist, so he knew nothing about the workings of the mind; and whilst he had a shelf in his house full of half-read business books and self-help books he'd never really understood why people think or do the things they do. But as he looked in the mirror that day he knew one thing for sure. Dreams are not real. They may represent things that could be created in the physical realm and that have the potential for life; and they could certainly influence the actions of people in the real world. But they were simply an idea which existed in people's imaginations. They could be incredibly powerful however; not necessarily in the mystical, magical 'think yourself to greatness' kind of way described in many self-help books, but because they become part of who you are. And therein lays the problem with the things that lazy optimists allow to converse with their heart; because they inhabit their waking dreams and tell stories which sound like they could develop into something exciting and wonderful; but are more likely to grow old and die in lonely isolation. The adversary of a dream is something which is equally unreal. It is another imagined, but extremely powerful force which has the potential to exist inside every person and can be allowed to grow or forced into a corner, depending on the grit and determination of its owner. The enemy of a dream is fear; and when fear wins the battle in the life of an optimist it results in laziness and inevitably leads to them being forced into ordinary, just like everyone else. (Not that there is anything wrong with that, if that is what you choose; but you must accept that it is your choice.)

That day, Charlie realised why it is that lazy optimists never take hold of their dreams. It is because while it still exists as a dream; that brightly illuminated banner of hope and certainty of what will one day come to be; that 'next big thing' or golden opportunity which is waiting just around the next corner ready to present itself, gift-wrapped, with your name on; then it is still true in the mind. It still has some semblance of reality which the optimistic mind can cling on to and strive for; a bit like placing all your hope on a lottery ticket. But fear tells them (quite correctly in truth) that if they try and fail then the dream dies too; and then what will they have to believe in; what will fuel their drive to carry on? But what fear hasn't told them is that the dream will die anyway if they don't pursue it and fight to make it a reality (because fear is always selective with the truth). And its passing will cause more pain, for longer, than it would if it went down in a blaze of attempted glory. Fear is also careful to miss out the undeniable fact that if you actually pursue your dream then it might just be a success and that the 'only' real hope of giving life to your dream is to get it out of your head and just go and do it. You genuinely do not have anything to lose.

LESSON 3:

"Don't just dream there… do something"

Charlie certainly wasn't a lazy man. He had worked hard all his life; and that day, as he stood in front of the mirror he didn't just beat himself up and make war on his inadequacies. He was honest enough to compliment all of the great attributes of the ordinary man too; his incredible ability to keep on going (even if he was fighting under a strategy of delusion) and the fact that whatever he put his hand to he had always worked hard at (even if it was misapplied effort). No, Charlie wasn't a lazy man at all; he had guts and fortitude in abundance; but he was lazy when it came to his dreams.

He learned that day that if he could identify exactly what the dream was; that thing which had lodged itself inside his heart and which had once burned brighter and warmer in his imagination than the sun on a perfect summer day; then he could actually go and pursue it. In the same way that he had avoided looking into his own eyes as he stood in front of the mirror, he had also been frightened to ever admit to himself that there were names and titles to his dreams. These collaborative creations of his own heart and mind were not just the stuff of fairy tales and picture books. They were not things which only ever happened to other people, lucky people, better people; he could identify them himself and actually go and achieve them; he could be successful.

You see Charlie believed that he was going to be successful. He believed that he was special and that one day he would rise above the mass of mediocrity which surrounded him, dragged him down and slowly drained him of his ambition; and then he would make a name for himself. He had always believed that success was an inescapable part of his future because Charlie had seized hold of a dream; and in this bright and colourful vision of his own destiny he saw himself winning. It had always been part of his nature to see life this way, to look beyond his present circumstances and see that tomorrow everything would be better; much, much better… but lazy optimism had always stood in his way.

Today, however, Charlie saw as plainly as the clear, bright, life-filled eyes which reflected hope back to him through the mirror, that he could go for his dream. And even if that particular dream never quite reached its potential then he could simply imagine greater ones and pursue those instead. You see Charlie had always been an optimist; but now he had determined in his heart that he would kill the lazy fear which had plagued him all of his life and let the 'active optimist' create and fulfil more dreams by the mindful.

Chapter 5

Charlie seizes the day…

The biggest battle of Charlie's entire life had taken place on the day that he had looked in the mirror, simply because it was a battle of equals; Charlie's dreams verses Charlie's fear. And as a result of that encounter he slept better that night than he had done in years; he had sweet dreams and in the morning his dreams awoke with him. And the next day became the day that Charlie's ambition left the corner of his mind it had occupied in varying degrees of lucidity since he was a child and became a solid object upon which he could climb high and stand tall. It was a platform which no longer faded into an air-filled, invisible vapour every time he awoke from his wistful, lazy slumber. Instead it had become a tall tower, standing amongst a battlement, dispelling any fear; because he finally knew that the only way to see if he really could be the person that he had always imagined himself to be was by taking hold of that desire with everything he had.

That day, the day Charlie's optimism turned into something far more substantial, was a day of action. You see, from that day onwards he didn't just 'have a dream' as other ordinary men dream, but rather he pursued one. And whilst it had been thinking, soul searching and a great deal of courageous honesty that had opened the door to the reality of his condition; he had learned from the experience that only deed and determination could take him through that door and towards the cure.

He summed up his transformation from lazy optimist to active optimist as the three INs which will help you OUT:

The first IN is for INFORMATION: Gaining this gives you the power to unlock the doors which stand between you and the various solutions or opportunities that you seek. It is important that you acquire the appropriate answers for the situation; but simply knowing the right information is never enough because knowledge is only power if you are able to wield it.

The second IN therefore is for INSPIRATION: This is the light bulb moment when you see how you can actually apply the information that you have in your possession. In other words you 'get it' so you can start to open the door which the previously acquired information had unlocked. To be inspired means to take action in your heart; not just in your head.

The final IN (is actually an IM) and is the one which will really help you OUT... it stands for

IMPLEMENTATION: Because an unlocked door is a start; an open door is an invitation; but only the act of actually walking through it can give you access to the solution or opportunity which is waiting for you on the other side.

So Charlie discovered that patience is not always a virtue; sometimes it is simply laziness. And that good things do not always come to those who wait; because those who go out and chase good things down usually get there first. And that is exactly what he did when he seized the day.

He took the ideas from his list of dreams which he had identified as the ones which still really mattered to him (there were only three) and he made a plan for each one of them. These plans grew, changed and developed in the days, weeks and months that followed; but there was enough substance written around each one on that first day that he could actually go and do something to get the dream out of his head and into the real world. This was important because until an action had taken place, all of the things which Charlie had fought for and reached into the loneliest depths of his heart for had no value at all. And he was determined on that day that he would not rest until he had carried out a positive deed to shatter the very concept of laziness that had haunted him for so long. First he examined each of these goals; the dreams which had wandered like shadows reflecting the various states of his mind for decades but which he had now allowed himself to visualise and virtualise onto paper. Boldly printed there, black ink against a pure white canvas, those ideas looked much less like fairy tales and more like ambitious, exciting projects which he was going to achieve. The next thing he did was to break down each vision into milestones or goalposts along the way; like spaces in a collectors' sticker book which needed to be filled. These spaces had absolute clarity attached to each one; personal details, positions, strengths, weaknesses and their place in the teamwork of the bigger ambition. Some of these gaps appeared more elusive than others, more difficult to identify a clear picture for or perhaps they were answers that might take longer to find. But as Charlie laid out the colourful plan before him and he observed the obstacles and openings which might appear in the future, he saw no fear and he saw no reason why he shouldn't be able to get back on the bike he had fallen from so many years before. Because this time he was working to a plan and it was a plan built around doing things today which moved him closer to tomorrow's goal.

With his dreams clearly classified onto paper and set out step by step in stages before him, the vast, untouchable terror of impossibility which had once masked their simplicity seemed so far away that he almost laughed at each one. He looked at the thing that he needed to do today in order to consider the day a success; and it was easy, it was simple, it was no more than a case of applying himself to a task. It was bold, because first steps always are, but incredibly easy and it formed the first bit of colour in a beautifully created, clearly stated and well-designed plan which declared "Charlie, you are a successful man" on every single page. Over the next few hours, as Charlie worked hard on that first task, making sure that he gave it his all and that it was the best it could possibly be, it occurred to him that it was as though he was distributing the first newspaper on a brand new paper round. He had a shiny new bike, with gears and good tyres ready to overcome any obstacle which might appear; he had planned his route before leaving the shop and he had brought his printout along to tell him where he needed to deliver next. With this happy analogy in his mind he realised that it had only ever been possible to open a single letterbox and deliver one paper at a time anyway; so he could never finish the round before he'd started. Carefully, paying very close attention to his plan to make sure he posted the right paper into the right door on the right street, he saw this first task through to completion and then peddled on to the next one. He smiled as he signed off the first deliverable piece of work on his journey to fulfilling a heart generated dream which, until then, had only ever possessed the potential to exist; but at that moment took the shape of foundation stones to a new reality.

In the weeks and months that followed Charlie made rapid progress towards his goals every single day. It was not always in leaps and bounds; sometimes there were small steps, occasionally side steps when things didn't quite go to plan and from time to time he even needed to adjust the direction of his stride completely. But he had a plan, he knew what he was aiming for and he knew each day what he needed to do to get him closer to it. So as long as he was applying the right amount of effort to the most appropriate steps for the situation he could earnestly tick each box as he went. And at the end of each day, as Charlie revisited his plan and saw that he had made progress towards it, he congratulated himself on his success and indulged himself in the thought that he was, quite literately, living the dream. And what's more he was living it on his terms; stepping closer and closer to his ultimate goals each day by simply taking ownership of an action which took him further along that road.

About a month after Charlie had taken the decision, and more importantly applied positive action, to giving life to his dreams he had really found his rhythm. It was at this time, when he was making such a steady beat of progress towards those goals that his natural talent for believing that he was special and destined to achieve great things was sounding out a clearer tune than ever before. His optimism was finally performing in perfect harmony with his work ethic and the sound that it produced was so beautiful and so powerful that it seemed to demand the magnificent crescendo that happened next. He resigned from his job.

In truth doing this was not a new thing, he had resigned from jobs many, many times before; usually on a whim and the promise of greener grass and brighter horizons in another pond which turned out to be muddier and more weed infested than the last. Because (as discussed before), symptoms of lazy optimism include a short span of attention, rapid descents into boredom and endlessly grasping at hopeless opportunities which just look like bright ideas. But this time it was different because the characteristics of healthy optimists, active optimists and

75

people like the new Charlie include laser-sharp focus, deliberate decisions, planned actions and the unwavering confidence to do what needs to be done.

It was on this day that Charlie reached the point in his plan which meant he needed to apply his effort full-time to the one of his dreams called 'I want to run my own business' (and the reality was that this day had arrived nearly two full months earlier than he had expected... such was the power of an optimist in possession of passion and a plan). And although this was seen by many of his colleagues, and indeed several members of his family, as another rash decision of a misguided dreamer who was once again destined to wander down the paths of mediocrity, it was in fact the safest and strongest career decision he had ever made. It was built upon the fact that Charlie had found comfort outside of his comfort zone and, although momentous and significant on many levels, in terms of action it was actually just a very small step in his journey toward a greater dream. And the structure, sound and movement of that journey, just like any perfectly written song, are the key elements which take its listener from one state to another. From one bar to the next, safely negotiating the high notes and low notes, past major twists and minor turns, over bridges, through changing tempos and finally delivering its message of hope and overcoming.

Charlie's 'I want to run my own business plan' had been born on the day he started his first paper round, but lay dormant beneath the burden of his increasingly heavy 'ordinary' life and his unwitting strive against a ticking clock. He had always known it was what he wanted to do, but it wasn't until he decided to actually do it that clarity on the 'what' arrived. And on the day that he lifted this aspiration from his list of dreams and began to build it into a plan, it became instantly obvious to him what his business should be. From this point on it genuinely was simple. Charlie planned, he took action, he started the business small to see if it would work and it did. He planned some more, he added scale, he reached the point where his income matched his salary and in handing in his notice that day he had taken the action which fulfilled a major part of that particular dream. It was as if magic filled his life for the first time since he had wished upon a star with his father, on a campsite, in a beautiful little seaside town, all that time ago. And here he was, so many years under his skin, with a family who he loved very much, in an average house with a good school for his kids and enough money to clothe them well and put food on the table. He had seen magic again that day and it delighted him; but he had also been reminded to appreciate the goodness that was all around him already and to keep his dreams attached to the things which mattered to him most.

Sometime later, as he examined the competition in his new marketplace and he saw the larger, more established businesses (the ones that looked a bit like Florida) he smiled to himself. He set a new target and made a plan. He decided that he would turn his business into a kind of Disneyland in the marketplace; a company to stand out from the rest, to be different and more focused on creating magic for its customers. And as he set that goal and designed the step by step, daily plan of actions which would get him there he realised that making and eating ice cream was far tastier than simply dreaming about it. Charlie's business went on to become a vehicle for the lifestyle he wanted for him and his family; working the hours he wanted to work and giving them all that they ever dreamed of or needed.

The second of Charlie's dreams took off in the same manner as the first. He measured it against his heart and found that it matched; he made a plan and on the first day, that day in which he had seized hold of his dreams, he took the first action towards giving it life. Of all of his dreams this one was the most outrageous, the most colourful and a veritable delight of dream-built fantasy and original thought beyond anything that anyone had ever attempted before. He was so excited at the potential it epitomised and when the patent office gave him a positive response he moved ahead with the plan; eager, enthusiastic, but still disciplined enough to take one step at a time. Then one day this particular dream failed. Its brightness faded, its promise jaded, and the practicalities of its construction simply disappeared forever. Charlie allowed himself some sadness; but he was too busy creating more dreams and taking actions which would fulfil his optimism to let disappointment reign for long. He looked back at the plan he had designed and it had been a good one; then examined the process to see what had gone wrong and there were lessons to learn for sure, but no blame to cast. And the conclusion of the matter, the sufficiency to soothe the suffering was that Charlie had rescued this dream from a dull death. It had languished in lazy abandon for decades until he had given it the chance of life; then it had exploded like a firework across a landscape of expectation and had showered those that saw it with the joy of potential.

So there was no lasting disappointment for Charlie in its life… because Charlie was an active optimist and he still had more dreams to pursue. Failure had become just another word; and not one that concerned him.

As for the third of the dreams which Charlie picked out from a lifetime of ambition and finally wrestled free from the grasp of a frightened, lazy optimist. Well you are reading it. This book, describes the genuine transition of an optimist who was afraid of his own ambition, into one that actually does something with his hopes and dreams. You see Charlie believes that optimism is a gift (and it is clear that not everyone has it) but he also knows that the majority of people who do possess this most valuable, noble and precious of personal attributes simply do not know how to use it. So if you think you are an optimist, particularly if you're beginning to identify yourself as a 'lazy' optimist; then please stop reading now and turn your gift into something that will get your dreams out of your head.

Epilogue:

Since the events described in this book (some of which are based on things which actually happened and some of which are completely made up) Charlie has continued to dream and imagine a whole host of "what could be?" ideas. He carefully supervises these dreams; but each time one catches a little bit more than his attention he applies the same process which resulted in getting the first few out of his head. So watch this space or find out more at:

www.lazyoptimist.co.uk

A final thought from a reformed lazy optimist:

"positive thinking is not as powerful as positive doing; it's just more attractive to lazy people"

About the Author

Martin Gladdish was born in Grantham, Lincolnshire but grew up in Tadley (a small town near Basingstoke) before moving to Hemel Hempstead where he lives with his wife Emma. He is a freelance copywriter and business coach; working with some of the UK's leading entrepreneurs to teach, mentor and support small businesses in implementing successful marketing and growth strategies.

Martin is a full-time Christian (meaning that his 'time' on this planet is 'full' because of Jesus Christ) and he is always willing to stop whatever he is doing to share the good news from the best book he has ever read. All you need to do is ask. You might wish you hadn't; but you absolutely should and it might just change your life too...

How can you create
a life that is truly
extraordinary?

What would be
possible if you
could?

A GUIDE TO LIVING ON PURPOSE WITH MEANING AND FREEDOM

In this extraordinarily helpful guide Ian Lock takes you through
the ideas, insights and explorations that will lead you to
answer these questions and more. The ambition here is no less
than to have you 'own and live the life you want'. So be
prepared to be provoked and challenged. And get ready to
shift your thinking and belief.

Recognised as a brilliant coach and consultant, Ian Lock is a
guide you can trust. Let him take you on an exploration into
what matters to you and how you can get more of what you
care about.

**'There are very few books that do what they say they do! This is a
powerful guide to anyone who wants more from their life -
read it! Go on and be extraordinary!"**
Anni Townend, Author of *Assertiveness and Diversity*

ISBN: 978-1-906954-70-3   Format: Paperback
Published: 3 January 2013   RRP: £12.99

DEVASTATED BY REDUNDANCY?

LEARN HOW TO USE THIS OPPORTUNITY TO CREATE A NEW AND BETTER LIFE FOR YOURSELF...

If you're one of the millions either already - or about to be - affected by redundancy, this book is for you.

It will enable you to:

- walk away from negative feelings of loss, despair, sadness;
- Understand that your occupational identity may be a thing of the past, but your unique identity isn't;
- Find the resources you need in this time of transition;
- Identify your new niche in life; and
- Develop positive and powerful ways of achieving it.

'This book is the next best thing to being coached by Elaine.
On Masterchef, contestants sometimes say "That's me on a plate".
This is Elaine in a book: warm, wise and witty. Best of all, parts of
the book are laugh out loud funny - and I wasn't expecting that.'
Redundancy coaching client

ISBN: 978-1-906954-55-0   Format: Paperback
Published: 16 October 2012   RRP: £18.99

Your step by step guide to

Winning Sales the Mindful Way
by developing:

- Relaxed Confidence
- Natural Performance
- Positive Partnerships
- Personal and Business Awareness
- Flexible Sales Process

*"When you discover relaxed confidence
and allow the sales process to flow naturally,
you will win sales without force."*
Steve Cox

ISBN: 978-1-906954-67-3   Format: Paperback
Published: 12 December 2012   RRP: £9.99

live it
PUBLISHING

Dreaming
of Being
Published

Inspiring Authors

Sought in the fields of MBS • Psychology
Health & Healing • Personal Development
NLP • Self-Help • Business • Leadership

www.liveitpublishing.com

Lightning Source UK Ltd.
Milton Keynes UK
UKHW021819040819
347384UK00002B/13/P